How to Build Trust in a Relationship

A FAQ Guide for Strengthening the Bond of Trust in a Relationship In Order to Enhance Peace and Development

Adegboye S. Aduragbemi

INTRODUCTION

Any successful marriage is based on trust since it is the foundation upon which love, intimacy, and a relationship are established. However, in the complex dance of marriage, concerns regarding how to develop, nurture, and uphold trust in the face of life's challenges frequently come up. "Trust FAQ in Marriage" is a helpful resource for married couples who are looking for clarification, comprehension, and valuable advice on building trust in their union.

This book contains a thorough list of frequently asked questions, thoughtful responses, and professional guidance specific to the subtleties of marriage-related trust. Couples may negotiate the landscape of trust with grace and intentionality by using practical tools, sensitivity, and understanding to address every question—from the delicate times of vulnerability to the difficulties of rebuilding trust after betrayal.

"Trust FAQ in Marriage" provides a road plan for couples to improve their connection, deepen their bond, and weather life's storms by using realistic tales, real-life events, and evidence-based techniques. Whether you're a newlywed looking to build trust or an experienced couple looking to strengthen your relationship, this book offers priceless insights and valuable strategies to help you deal with the challenges of trust with resilience and confidence.

May you find comfort in other people's experiences that you have shared, inspiration in the knowledge of professionals, and the bravery to accept trust as a means of achieving a higher level of fulfilment and connection in your marriage as you set out on this path of research and discovery.

Together, let's explore the ageless issues, complex dynamics, and exquisite beauty of marital trust.

Chapter One

Fixing Trust in Your Relationship

When Trust Fails

There was a time when Emily and David lived together in the charming village of Oakwood. Their mutual interests and strong chemistry brought them together when they were in college. Though on the surface, their love story appeared to be straight out of a fairy tale, cracks were starting to show.

Emily was a sweet, compassionate nurse who had entire faith in David. She never questioned his dedication or honesty since she knew he was devoted to her and loved her. David was an attractive businessman with a captivating demeanour who delighted in Emily's devotion, feeling the warmth of her unshakable faith.

But as their relationship developed, Emily started to have doubts about David because of his frequent business travels and late-night office work. At first, she wrote off her misgivings as the product of her anxieties and inadequacies. But Emily started to lose faith in David as he became increasingly withdrawn and reticent.

Emily found proof of David's adultery one fateful day when she noticed several damning texts on his phone. Heartbroken and devastated, she confronted him and demanded an explanation and responsibility. David, realizing his trick, apologized and made amends, but his words were ignored.

The weight of their problems caused Emily and David's relationship to fall apart as they were unable to make sense of the betrayal and loss of trust. Desperate to save their marriage, they attempted communication exercises, couples counselling, and even a brief separation, but to no avail. Ultimately, they both lamented the loss of the love they had once had and made the painful choice to separate ways.

Years later, Emily and David coincidentally crossed paths once more. They couldn't help but feel a twinge of grief for the love they had lost as they made small talk. They realized that their relationship had been ruined by a lack of trust and regretted not prioritizing openness, honesty, and communication earlier.

This narrative shows how trust difficulties may undermine even the most solid relationships, emphasizing the value of openness, sincerity, and respect for one another in building strong, long-lasting bonds.

Power of Trust

Emily and Daniel were two people whose paths unexpectedly intersected in the charming town of Willowbrook, subsequent in a partnership built on mutual respect and trust. They first connected at a neighbourhood charity function where Daniel, a generous philanthropist with a love of helping people, and Emily, a volunteer coordinator committed to improving her town, collaborated on several initiatives.

They bonded via their shared ideals and dedication to giving back, which made their early contacts friendly and cheerful. Daniel was enthralled with Emily's unwavering commitment and compassion, while Emily appreciated Daniel's honesty and integrity.

Emily and Daniel found a profound understanding and connection as they spent more time together, which went beyond simple friendship. They established a foundation of openness and trust in their developing relationship by sharing their dreams, worries, and hopes with one another.

As they negotiated life's ups and downs together, their shared dedication to honesty and integrity became the foundation of their connection. Daniel had complete faith in Emily to support and encourage him in all of his undertakings, and Emily had complete faith in Daniel to always act in her best interests.

Their mutual respect and everlasting trust gave them strength and comfort when they needed it most, and their relationship grew as a result. Emily and Daniel supported one another through everything, trusting in the strength of their relationship, whether it was dealing with difficulties at work, conquering personal barriers, or enjoying life's little pleasures.

As their love grew, Emily and Daniel committed themselves to one another by exchanging vows in front of loved ones in a touching ceremony. Acknowledging that trust was the cornerstone of their relationship and the secret to their happiness; they embraced it between them.

Years later, Emily and Daniel reflected on their adventure with delight and thankfulness. They were appreciative of the love and support they had found in one another. They understood that their relationship had been based on a basic foundation of honesty, trust, and respect for one another. With trust serving as their compass, they felt their love would endure for many more years to come. Their link had only gotten stronger with time.

This story shows how trust may be the cornerstone of a relationship. It emphasizes the value of openness, sincerity, and respect for one another in creating a solid and enduring alliance.

Chapter Two

Synopsis for Communication

What is trust, and why is it crucial in a marriage?

Mutual respect, honesty, and dependability are the cornerstones of a strong and wholesome marriage, and trust is the cornerstone of these qualities. It entails having faith in your spouse's moral character, goals, and reliability in fulfilling promises. In a relationship, trust cultivates emotional intimacy, security, and a sense of cooperation.

After a betrayal or fracture in our marriage, how can we mend the trust?

Following a betrayal or breach, trust must be rebuilt via honest conversation, mutual responsibility, and a commitment to healing. Setting limits, apologizing, recognizing the harm, and cooperating to resolve underlying problems are some steps in the process. Rebuilding trust takes time and can be aided by consistent behaviours that show dependability, integrity, and transparency.

How do we handle common indicators of trust concerns in marriages?

Suspicion, jealousy, a lack of communication, and trouble depending on your partner are typical indicators of trust issues. Prioritize direct and honest communication, respect one another's emotions, and collaborate to find and resolve underlying problems in order to fix trust issues. To properly handle trust concerns, get help from a therapist or counsellor if necessary.

How can we strengthen our marriage by honest and open communication?

Communicating with your spouse in an open, sincere, and vulnerable manner is vital to developing trust. Embrace empathy, nonjudgmental communication, and active listening to establish a secure environment for candid discussion. Openly express your feelings, ideas, and worries to your partner, and urge them to do the same.

How can we foster forgiveness in our marriage, and what part does forgiveness play in restoring trust?

Following a betrayal or break of trust, forgiveness is crucial to restoring confidence. Develop forgiveness by empathizing with others, letting go of grudges, and concentrating on your mutual healing and forward motion. When required, extend heartfelt regrets, accept accountability, and make a long-term commitment to restoring trust via regular acts and behaviours.

Chapter Three

Issues regarding a few more essential elements that significantly impact marital communication

What are some ways to keep trust complications out of our marriage in the first place?

From the start of your relationship, putting honesty, integrity, and communication first will help prevent trust issues. Keep your word, be open and honest with your spouse, and resolve problems or disagreements quickly and amicably. To encourage trust in your marriage, establish a foundation of respect, understanding, and dependability between you both.

How can we resolve trust issues in our marriage that are a result of trauma or past experiences?

It takes time, empathy, and assistance from both partners to navigate trust challenges resulting from trauma or past experiences. Establish a safe environment for candid communication, respect one another's emotions and worries, and collaborate to resolve underlying problems as you progressively increase trust.

If we are lacking trust because of relationships or experiences from the past, what should we do?

If your marriage is suffering from a lack of trust as a result of previous interactions or experiences, give open communication, empathy, and reassurance top priority. Talk to your partner about any unresolved fears or insecurities, get help from a therapist or counsellor if necessary, and cooperate in developing trust over time progressively.

How do we resolve trust issues in our marriage that stem from regrets or past transgressions?

Resolving trust issues resulting from past errors or regrets requires openness, sensitivity, and a readiness to grow and learn from the experience. Admit any mistakes or regrets, show sincere regret, and promise to change for the better as we advance. As you work through the fallout from previous mistakes together, exercise patience, empathy, and forgiveness.

In order to foster trust in our marriage, how can we give each other a sense of safety and assurance?

Giving dependability, consistency, and transparency a top priority in your actions and behaviours is necessary to instil a sense of security and assurance. Remain dependable, fulfil your end of the bargain, and be forthright and honest in your communication with your spouse. Regularly express your love, gratitude, and admiration for one another to strengthen the sense of security and trust that permeates your partnership.

As our marriage develops over time, how can we foster trust in it?

It takes constant work and dedication from both partners to maintain trust in your marriage. Maintain an ongoing emphasis on honesty, open communication, and transparency in all of your dealings. To keep mistrust from growing, communicate often, show gratitude and appreciation, and resolve issues or disagreements right away.

If one partner has acted dishonestly or in violation of boundaries, how can we mend that trust?

Following boundary violations or dishonest behaviour, trust must be rebuilt through openness, responsibility, and a partner's resolve to make amends. In order to restore confidence, the offending partner must accept accountability for their actions, be open to making apologies, and focus on acting with constant honesty and integrity. The betrayed partner needs to be prepared to communicate honestly, establish and uphold firm boundaries, and give the other partner a chance to win back their trust through deeds.

How can we foster vulnerability in our marriage, and what part does vulnerability play in the development of trust?

Since vulnerability encourages closeness, connection, and authenticity, it is crucial for establishing trust in a married relationship. Generate a benign space for your partner to share their thoughts, feelings, and fears with you in order to cultivate vulnerability. Over time, strengthen your relationship and develop trust by engaging in nonjudgmental support, empathy, and active listening.

Chapter Four

Maintaining equilibrium within a married relationship

How can we deal with inadequacy or insecurity feelings that could undermine trust in our marriage?

Acknowledging and accepting oneself requires cultivating self-awareness, self-compassion, and self-acceptance. Openly discuss your feelings with your partner, ask for comfort when you need it, and collaborate to support one another and foster a good self-image.

What are some doable actions we can do every day to build trust in our marriage?

Making dependability, consistency, and openness a priority in your acts and behaviours is essential to building trust in your marriage. Remain dependable, fulfil your end of the bargain, and be forthright and honest in your communication with your spouse. Regularly express your gratitude, respect, and admiration for one another to strengthen your bond of trust.

If one partner has previously acted dishonestly or unfaithfully, how can we mend that trust?

After deceit or adultery, trust must be rebuilt with patience, work, and a shared commitment to recovery from both parties. It could entail apologizing, admitting wrongdoing, and offering compensation. While the betrayed partner needs to rebuild trust and work through feelings of betrayal gradually, the offending partner needs to show genuine remorse, transparency, and accountability. Therapy or counselling might help you through this challenging journey.

What steps should we take to address trust issues resulting from cultural or religious differences?

Resolving trust issues resulting from cultural or religious disparities calls for empathy, honest communication, and a desire to grow as a community. To foster trust and understanding in your marriage, find common ground, be open and respectful of each other's views and values, and communicate honestly about your opinions.

What are some widespread myths regarding marital trust, and how can we dispel them?

Commonly held misconceptions about trust include the ideas that it ought to be automatic, that once it's lost, it can never be gained, and that it always needs to be fully transparent. Dispel these myths by emphasizing open communication, empathy, and forgiveness in your relationship and by realizing that trust is developed gradually via consistent acts and behaviours.

How can we strengthen our marriage's foundation of trust in the face of uncertainty or change?

Resilience, adaptability, and a willingness to change together are necessary for fostering trust in uncertain or changing times. Make empathy, open communication, and mutual support your top priorities. Reassure each other of your commitment to the relationship. As a team, navigate challenges and uncertainties by leaning on each other for support and assurance.

If one partner has not fulfilled commitments or broken promises, how can we mend the trust?

Holding the offending partner accountable, dependable, and consistent is necessary to rebuild trust following broken promises or unfulfilled commitments. The guilty party needs to own up to their errors, offer heartfelt apologies, and take proactive measures to prove their dependability and fulfil their end of the bargain. The partner who has been betrayed must be prepared to set clear expectations for future behaviour and be willing to forgive and move past feelings of disappointment.

How do we deal with trust issues stemming from unresolved issues in our marriage or previous conflicts?

Resolving trust issues stemming from previous disputes or outstanding matters necessitates tolerance, comprehension, and a shared dedication to finding a solution from both parties. Schedule time for direct and honest communication, acknowledge each other's emotions and collaborate to gradually restore trust by addressing underlying problems. If you find it challenging to work through trust issues on your own, think about getting outside assistance from a therapist or counsellor.

If one partner experiences jealousy or insecurity, how do we deal with trust issues?

Handling jealousy or insecurity-related trust issues calls for tolerance, comfort, and understanding from both parties. Establish a secure environment where people can talk freely about their emotions and worries. Then, work together to overcome underlying fears and develop trust gradually. Use compassion, affirmation, and consolation to help one another when you're feeling uncertain or uneasy.

How can we resolve trust issues in our marriage that are caused by past traumas or betrayals?

Both partners must exhibit sensitivity, compassion, and patience in order to resolve trust issues resulting from past traumas or betrayals. Establish a safe environment where people can talk freely about their past experiences, accept one another's hurt and emotions, and gradually rebuild trust through support, communication, and consistent behaviour.

What are some doable tactics for fostering trust in a remote marriage?

Prioritizing communication, transparency, and dependability is essential to developing trust in a long-distance marriage. Schedule regular check-ins through messaging, video chats, or phone calls, and be open and truthful about your feelings and experiences. Despite the distance, build trust by being dependable and consistent, keeping your word, and honouring your word.

How do we rebuild trust if one partner has consistently violated boundaries or disregarded the other's feelings and needs?

Rebuilding trust after consistently violating boundaries or disregarding feelings and needs requires significant effort, accountability, and a commitment to change from the offending partner. The angry partner must take responsibility for their actions, apologize sincerely, and demonstrate genuine efforts to respect boundaries and prioritize their partner's feelings and needs. The betrayed spouse must be willing to communicate their boundaries clearly, set consequences for repeated violations, and be open to rebuilding trust gradually as they see consistent efforts and change from their partner.

How can we prevent trust difficulties from harming our capacity to discuss and resolve conflicts in our marriage correctly?

Preventing trust difficulties from impacting communication and conflict resolution entails stressing open communication, active listening, and empathy. Make time for regular check-ins to address feelings, worries, and problems honestly, and be willing to validate each other's viewpoints and find mutually acceptable solutions. Establish a foundation of trust and sympathy to negotiate disagreements constructively and enhance your bond as partners.

Chapter Five

Protecting your union from unrecognized influences

In the event of a privacy violation, like spying on one another's gadgets or accounts, how can we regain each other's trust?

Following a privacy violation, trust must be rebuilt through openness, responsibility, and a shared commitment to honouring each other's limits. Discuss the breach honestly and openly, offer a sincere apology if needed, and set forth clear guidelines and expectations for privacy as we advance in your partnership.

What are some red flags that our marriage might be suffering because of trust issues?

Frequent disagreements or arguments, a lack of emotional closeness or communication, and feelings of mistrust or jealousy are warning signs of trust issues. Observe how your relationship is changing, and take quick action to resolve any worries or problems to keep trust issues from getting worse.

How can we keep trust issues from interfering with our marriage's other facets, like communication or intimacy?

Dealing with worries or disagreements in a timely and positive manner is essential to preventing trust issues from impacting other areas of your marriage. Make empathy, attentive listening, and open communication your top priorities to avoid miscommunication and resentment from growing. To bolster trust and resilience in your marriage, work on improving other aspects of your relationship, such as intimacy and connection.

How can we resolve trust issues in our marriage that concern money or joint property?

Maintaining shared financial goals and values, accountability, and transparency are essential in navigating trust issues pertaining to finances. Establish clear expectations and boundaries, have frank discussions about your financial status, and collaborate to develop an economic and financial strategy that takes into account the needs and priorities of both partners.

What are some tools or resources that we can use to improve our marriage's trust?

Take into account reading books or articles about developing trust in relationships, going to seminars or workshops on communication and trust-building techniques, or getting help from a counsellor or therapist with a focus on couples therapy. To strengthen trust and connection in your marriage, make self-awareness, empathy, and active listening a priority in your daily interactions with your spouse.

How do we handle warning signs that point to a lack of trust in our marriage?

Cliques about a lack of trust can include defensiveness, accusations all the time, secrecy, and a refusal to discuss issues honestly. By placing a high value on honest communication, confirming each other's emotions, and making an effort to comprehend the root causes of mistrust, you can address these warning signs.

How do we mend trust in our marriage following a significant breach, like adultery or financial betrayal?

Following a severe breach, trust needs to be rebuilt. In order to get this done, both parties must be committed, transparent, and willing to address underlying problems. The partner who violated the relationship needs to own up to their mistakes, show sincere regret, and work steadily to regain the other person's trust by being trustworthy, dependable, and accountable. When the betrayed partner notices consistent efforts and changes from their partner, they should be willing to work through their feelings of betrayal and pain, seek support when needed, and gradually reopen their eyes to trust.

How do we deal with trust issues stemming from unresolved issues in our marriage or previous conflicts?

Resolving trust issues stemming from previous disputes or outstanding matters necessitates tolerance, comprehension, and a shared dedication to finding a solution from both parties. Schedule time for direct and honest communication, acknowledge each other's emotions and collaborate to gradually restore trust by addressing underlying problems. If you find it challenging to work through trust issues on your own, think about getting outside assistance from a therapist or counsellor.

If one partner has a substance use disorder or substance abuse, how can we establish trust again?

When one partner battles addiction or substance abuse, repairing trust necessitates a multifaceted strategy that includes counselling, support groups, and potentially professional treatment. The addicted partner needs to actively participate in their recovery by going to treatment or support group meetings, communicating openly about their progress, and making steady attempts to stay sober. To safeguard themselves and progressively reestablish trust, the other partner must be understanding and supportive while establishing reasonable boundaries.

How do we resolve trust issues in our marriage with regard to privacy, social media, and boundaries?

It takes open communication, mutual respect, and a willingness to set and respect each other's boundaries to address trust issues with social media, privacy, and boundaries. Have honest conversations about your concerns and expectations regarding social media usage, privacy settings, and online interactions. To foster trust and preserve a harmonious balance in your relationship, be open and honest about your online activities and show respect for one another's personal space.

If one partner has compromised the other's trust or disclosed private information without authorization, how can we mend that trust?

Rebuilding trust after betraying confidence or sharing sensitive information without consent requires sincere apologies, accountability, and dedication to the transformation of trust through consistent actions. The offending partner must acknowledge their mistake, express genuine remorse, and demonstrate respect for their partner's boundaries and privacy.

31

The partner involved in the betrayal must be willing to express their emotional state, set clear boundaries, and give the offending partner the opportunity to earn back their trust through transparent and respectful behaviour over time.

How can we prevent trust issues from affecting our ability to parent effectively as a team?

Preventing trust issues from affecting your ability to parent effectively involves prioritizing open communication, mutual respect, and shared decision-making. Make time for regular check-ins to discuss parenting goals, concerns, and strategies, and be willing to compromise and support each other's parenting styles. Establish a robust platform of trust and cooperation in your co-parenting relationship to foster a supportive and harmonious environment for your children.

How do we address trust issues related to financial matters, such as spending habits or financial transparency?

Addressing trust issues related to finances requires open communication, honesty, and a willingness to work together as a team. Create a budget together, discuss financial goals and priorities, and be transparent about your spending habits and financial decisions. Set clear expectations for financial transparency and accountability, and be willing to address concerns or conflicts promptly and constructively to rebuild trust and strengthen your economic partnership.

How can we rebuild trust if one partner has been emotionally unavailable or distant in our marriage?

Rebuilding trust after emotional distance or unavailability requires efforts from both partners to reconnect and foster emotional intimacy. The partner who has been emotionally distant must be willing to open up, communicate openly, and demonstrate genuine interest and empathy towards their partner's feelings and needs. The other partner must be patient and understanding while expressing their feelings and needs and providing reassurance that they are willing to work through the challenges together.

How do we rebuild trust after a breach of privacy, such as going through each other's devices without consent?

Rebuilding trust after a breach of privacy requires acknowledgement of the violation, sincere apologies, and a commitment to respecting each other's boundaries. Both partners must discuss their feelings about privacy and establish clear boundaries regarding personal space and devices. The offending partner must demonstrate a willingness to respect boundaries and rebuild trust through transparent actions. In contrast, the other partner must be willing to forgive and work towards rebuilding trust gradually.

How do we address trust issues if one partner has a history of lying or deception in our marriage?

Addressing trust issues related to lying or deception requires honesty, transparency, and a commitment to change from the dishonest partner. The dishonest partner must acknowledge their past behaviour, express genuine remorse, and be willing to be open and honest moving forward. The other partner must be willing to communicate their feelings and concerns openly, set clear expectations for honesty, and give the dishonest partner the opportunity to earn back their trust through consistent actions.

How can we rebuild trust after breaches in confidentiality, such as sharing private information with others without consent?

Rebuilding trust after breaches in confidentiality requires sincere apologies, accountability, and a commitment to respecting each other's privacy. The partner who breached confidentiality must acknowledge their mistake, express genuine remorse, and take steps to rebuild trust by respecting boundaries and maintaining confidentiality moving forward. The other partner must be willing to communicate their feelings and concerns, set clear boundaries, and give the offending partner the opportunity to demonstrate respect for their privacy.

How do we address trust issues if one partner has consistently failed to keep promises or commitments in our marriage?

Addressing trust issues related to broken promises or unfulfilled commitments requires accountability, reliability, and a commitment to change from the unreliable partner. The unreliable partner must acknowledge their past behaviour, express genuine remorse, and take steps to rebuild trust by consistently following through on promises and commitments. The other partner must be willing to communicate their feelings and concerns, set clear expectations for reliability, and give the unreliable partner the opportunity to earn back their trust through consistent actions.

How can we prevent trust issues from affecting our ability to make joint decisions or plans for the future?

Preventing trust concerns from hurting decision-making and preparing for the future needs open communication, mutual respect, and a willingness to engage as partners. Make time for regular discussions about goals, priorities, and plans for the future, and be willing to compromise and support one other's dreams. Create a solid background for trust and cooperation in order to navigate decisions and plans together effectively.

How do we address trust concerns due to unresolved fights or lingering resentments in our marriage?

Addressing trust issues due to unsolved conflicts or resentments needs time, understanding, and a commitment to settlement from both partners. Make time for open and honest communication about previous disagreements, acknowledge each other's feelings and viewpoints, and work together to find solutions and closure. Practice forgiveness, empathy, and a readiness to let go of grudges to repair trust and deepen your relationship.

How can we preserve trust in our marriage as we handle changes in roles, duties, or situations throughout time?

Maintaining trust in your marriage during changes in roles, duties, or circumstances demands adaptability, flexibility, and a commitment to communication from both spouses. Make time for regular discussions about expectations, concerns, and needs as roles and circumstances shift, and be open to support one another through transitions and problems. Lean on each other for emotional support, acknowledge each other's feelings, and display reliability and consistency to establish trust and resilience in your relationship.

Shielding your union from outside impacts

How do we deal with trust issues resulting from family dynamics or relationships in the past?

It takes empathy and understanding on the part of both partners to resolve trust issues that are the result of previous relationships or family dynamics. Establish a safe environment where people can talk freely about their past experiences, accept one another's emotions, and collaborate to establish healthy boundaries and trust progressively.

How do we maintain trust in our marriage as external stressors and life changes occur?

Maintaining trust in your marriage during external stressors and life changes involves prioritizing open communication, mutual support, and flexibility. Make time for regular check-ins to discuss concerns and challenges, and be eager to familiarize and adjust as needed to navigate changes together. Lean on each other for emotional support, validate each other's feelings, and demonstrate reliability and consistency to reinforce trust and strengthen your bond during difficult times.

How do we address trust issues if one partner has a history of infidelity or has cheated in the past?

Addressing trust issues related to infidelity or past cheating requires open communication, honesty, and a commitment to rebuilding trust from both partners. The spouse who cheated must take responsibility for their actions, express genuine remorse, and be willing to answer questions and provide reassurance to their partner. The betrayed partner must be willing to express their feelings, set clear boundaries, and work through feelings of betrayal with support from their partner.

About the Author

ADEGBOYE S. ADURAGBEMI is a manager, business administrator, entrepreneur, and motivational speaker in Africa. ADEGBOYE has his BA from Yale University, IPMA from Adonai University, and a Masters in Business Administration (MBA) from the University of Salford, Manchester.

He was born in South Africa but is presently based in Nigeria as a motivational speaker and marriage counsellor in institutions, sectors, and seminars with young and upcoming managers all over Africa.

Acknowledgements

I want to express my sincere gratitude to everyone who helped with the "FAQ on Communication in Marriage." Throughout this journey, their encouragement, insight, and support have been priceless.

I want to start by acknowledging the fact that, without God, this guide wouldn't have been possibly achieved.

And also to my spouse, who has always been motivating and supportive in making this task successful, I will always love and appreciate you.

I have many couples to appreciate who have shared their experiences, challenges, and victories with me over the years. Your openness, weakness, and tenacity have enhanced the book's pages and provided priceless insights into the difficulties of marriage communication.

My sincere gratitude goes out to my family and friends for their continuous support and encouragement during this journey. Your wise advice, tolerance, and words of support have helped me get through the complicated process of writing and releasing this book.

I sincerely thank the specialists and experts who have so kindly offered their knowledge and skills in marriage and communication. Your advice and thoughts have improved this book's quality and depth, and I really appreciate your contributions.

Finally, I would like to express my profound gratitude to all of the readers of this work. As you journey through the process of communication in your marriage, I hope that the knowledge, direction, and encouragement provided within these pages will be a source of inspiration and empowerment for you.

I sincerely appreciate your help.